T0149575

THE BEST WORKOUT IS
"SEX"

A Gay Guide to Your Ideal Marriage

ALVIN LOPEZ-WOODS
&
ANTONIO LOPEZ-WOODS

authorHOUSE®

AuthorHouse™
1663 Liberty Drive
Bloomington, IN 47403
www.authorhouse.com
Phone: 1-800-839-8640

Published by AuthorHouse   03/21/2012

ISBN: 978-1-4685-6317-7 (sc)
ISBN: 978-1-4685-6316-0 (e)

Library of Congress Control Number: 2012904692

Any people depicted in stock imagery provided by Thinkstock are models, and such images are being used for illustrative purposes only.
Certain stock imagery © Thinkstock.

This book is printed on acid-free paper.

CONTENTS

Alvin and Antonio were recently married in New York State on the first day of legal same-sex unions. The couple provides overarching relationship advice for both heterosexual and same-sex couples.

DEDICATION

This book is dedicated to our families. Thank you for the support, through it all . . . .

Manny Andino, we've worked on this project in your memory. Love you. Rest in perfection.

EPIGRAPH

"For it was not into my ear you whispered, but into my heart. It was not my lips you kissed, but my soul."

Judy Garland

PREFACE

We are a young, same-sex couple that hopes to enlighten heterosexual and same-sex couples, alike on ways to turn a healthy relationship into a solid marriage. The mission of *The Best Workout is "Sex": A Gay Guide to Your Ideal Marriage* is to shine a spotlight on love and respect being vital to any union, regardless of gender and sexual orientation. We're optimistic that sharing the intimate tips and personal learnings that have guided us to *our* ideal relationship will give you the needed confidence to make your romantic partnership successful.

ACKNOWLEDGEMENT

This project not only strengthened our bond but also has reinforced our connection with people, organizations, and groups that have pioneered human rights and marriage equality for all. We do not take it lightly that we stand on the shoulders of prolific greatness.

First, we would like to thank every person that sent us their best wishes and extended blessings on our union. It is because of all of you that have optimistically journeyed throughout our lives that we find the courage to live in our own truth.

The Gay & Lesbian Alliance Against Defamation, (GLAAD). Your mission to amplify the voice of the LGBT community through empowering real people to share their stories has been the single most important example to us. Your relentless promotion of understanding as well as the push to increase acceptance within our community has guided us into the individuals that we have aspired to be.

Human Rights Campaign, (HRC). Standing at the forefront of individual state battles for marriage equality is why we were able to legally wed and change our last name to Lopez-Woods. The joining of our last names to "create our own family" is truly one of our biggest accomplishments. We will forever be indebted to your dedication for change in the state of New York.

To Dan Savage and Terry Miller. Creating the "It Gets Better Project" was truly a moment in history that reshaped the mindset of people around the world. It is because of your efforts that our heterosexual allies also have a dominate voice to pioneer change along with us. Your campaign has instilled hope within young LGBT people while bringing an intense awareness to the difficult growing pains that gay teens face. We all want to grow up, find a person to love, and be happy. Supporters around the world are making the lives of people just like us, a lot brighter. We appreciate all that you do.

To Judge Gerald Lebovitz, you legally made our marriage official. Bless you, sir.

INTRODUCTION
Elle-Woods

At our core, all we want is to be loved. Human beings are bonded by an intense nature to share this journey of life with the person who will love them unconditionally. People fall in love, feverishly plan a wedding, and seal the deal with a ceremonial kiss *but* don't think about the most important part of the union—after the honeymoon. What comes after the kiss that links you to your spouse for better or worse? The answer—enduring selfless work.

In an era of pop culture where media all but rejoices in less than one-hundred day unions of celebrities, it is easy to forget that marriage is a celebration of love and commitment. Marriage is a civil right in which all adult couples should be able to enter wholeheartedly. Most fail to realize that marriage is hard work! As love between two people deepens, the bond of marriage strengthens. Often times the satisfaction of wedded bliss begins to decline for various reasons. If you are starting to feel displeasure in your union, ask yourself this question—What am I doing to replenish the nutrients that make up my relationship? A partnership between two adults has to be nourished in order to thrive.

Contrary to the title of the book, this collection of tips and writing focuses on several facets of two people in a relationship, other than the physical act of sex. *The Best Workout is "Sex": A Gay Guide to Your Ideal Marriage* magnifies what makes physical love between a couple so intense—emotional and mental connections. Think about it, you and your partner should be having some form of *sex* at all times that excludes the physical act. The intimate journey of learning to connect with your partner in love is the ultimate fuel for a successful marriage.

In today's inclusive world it is imperative that both gay and straight couples alike are aware of certain guidelines to build toward a healthy relationship. After all, more and more same-sex couples are gaining the right to wed just like their heterosexual counterparts. It is our hope that this book will teach you reliable tips to enhance the connection with your soon to be spouse, husband or wife. Regardless of whom your heart belongs too, the focus here is the overarching theme of love and respect—two principles that we crave in humanity. Our goal was to create a blueprint, or sorts, that can be used for all couples since relationships are a constant learning process.

We are often asked, "Who plays the dominate role in your relationship?" or the most dreaded question, "You are dealing with another man so how could you possibly understand?" The reality is—we completely understand! What many people fail to realize is that most successful relationships have parallel components. Loving another person is just that—love. As a couple, we share the same values and morals of the straight couple next door. The only difference is we are two attractive men.

In advance of our collection of thoughts, we would like you to get better acquainted with us. We're Mr. and *Mr.* Lopez-Woods, a young couple, ferociously in love, and living everyday together as if it were the last. Our evolving collective identity is a modern-American truth—two guys from different backgrounds, balancing an intense relationship that led to a trailblazing marriage in New York City on Sunday, July, 24, 2011—the first day of legalized same-sex unions in New York State.

Elle-Woods Personal Note from Alvin:

I found it extremely difficult as a young boy growing up in Louisiana, knowing that many people did not share my personal views on life. Not only did I have to privately deal with being sexually attracted to men, I also struggled with the excruciating reality that I was a mother-less child. My biological mother chose to not be a part of my life when I was six-years old and that decision shaped the man that I have become. Often times, I was my own worst enemy and never thought that I would get to a point in life where I would be comfortable living in my own truth.

I made the best effort to keep people emotionally detached from me until I made the definitive choice to be happy. That fateful moment in college drastically changed my perception on what it is to love and be loved. One of my primary objectives in life is to bring an encouraging awareness to those who struggle with being who they are because of the love, or lack thereof, in their lives. Making a choice to unconditionally love myself afforded me the opportunity of a lifetime—to meet, pursue, and marry the love of my life.

Elle-Woods Personal Note from Antonio:

Being the eldest son in my family was a bit challenging, since I grew up not feeling as if I could be myself. Most of my life, a guard was up because I knew that I was different from my five brothers and feared that my different would not be accepted. The reality of my sexual orientation mentally burned a hole in my spirit throughout my adolescent years. It wasn't until I was a teenager that I realized it was time to make a personal change for my own well-being. Now free of all self-inflicted hatred and no longer scared of what people thought of me, I finally became happy.

I've always loved the idea of being in love as well as being around people who were affectionate and were not afraid to show it. I hold sincere admiration for my parents, who have weathered the storm and never gave up on loving one another or their family. With a clear mindset of the man that I was growing into, my life-long urge to fall in love finally had an outlet. Now my heart yearned for the answers to two important questions—Who would love me? What would it feel like to be in love? Once I became comfortable with loving myself I was able to find and marry my true love.

Before we get started on this lesson of guiding you on how to connect both mentally and emotionally with your partner, you have to be open to this important statement—happiness is a choice. Have you made a choice to make your relationship work? Have you decided to make a full commitment to doing the arduous work needed to make your marriage last?

Now that the preliminary questions are out of the way and everyone is on one accord, we can divulge learnings from our perspective that will surely enhance the connection between you and your husband, wife or soon-to-be spouse. Let's get started!

CHAPTER I

Love You
or
Heart You

Prior to exploring a relationship, work to discover you. Far too often, people fail to realize the importance of loving themselves before successfully being able to love another person. We all share the common need to be loved and are quick to find gratification with that at-the-moment someone for all the wrong reasons. The cosmic journey of a romantic relationship is difficult enough when all the stars are aligned, so imagine the treacherous voyage ahead if you are not in love—with you.

Fall in Love with the Person You See in the Mirror Every Day. It sounds simple to do, right? Sadly, it's not that easy. Self-hatred can cause you to make horrible decisions in life, especially with matters of the heart. Loving yourself can be a daunting task when you feel like you are not worthy of such affection. Work to overcome personal speed bumps and realize that you are much stronger than the burdens that dwarf your progress.

To build love within, start each and every day by motivating yourself with personal words of encouragement. You'll probably have some difficulty nourishing your own spirit at the beginning of this exercise but the personal relationship builder with yourself will soon become second nature. Being in a comfortable state of reassuring yourself is an essential sign that you are indeed falling in love with the person you see in the mirror.

Once the confidence boosting mirror exercise is mastered, personal worth and self-esteem will surely blossom. Take this into consideration—if you can't stand your own company, it's a guarantee that those who associate with you will share the same difficulty.

The Person You Want to Become. Now that your self-assurance is headed in the right direction, it's time to focus on who you are as well as the person you want to be. Find it within yourself to develop realistic goals that will lead you toward the person you want to become. Without attainable plans, there is no way to truly pinpoint where you're going. Think about this—mature people seeking solid relationships tend to want someone that has a personal plan to succeed as well as a plan of action.

Don't Bring Negative Experiences of Your Past into the Present. Living in a moment of irrationality, due to clouded thoughts of a stormy past, is easy. You must change your thought process in order to get through dark moments that have happened in life. It can become downright annoying for your significant other to deal with a person, who consistently plays the victim by overreacting to situations solely based on what they have previously experienced.

Be Gentle with You. Everyone has a story and may think that their situation is far worse than the next person. Get real. Stop milking the victim role by meandering in the past and jump into the present, or you will remain stagnant in life and love. Working to alter your perception of life will definitely be a challenge. With that being said, it can be accomplished. Do your best to not beat yourself up if the changes you want in life aren't coming to fruition as fast as you may have hoped. If you can't let go of the past in the very moment, don't worry your fragile heart. Be gentle enough with yourself to embark on a life changing excursion and your time will come.

Loving yourself before you can attempt to romantically love someone else is an absolute must.

CHAPTER II

The Art of Support

Relationships are best when both partners are a vital support system for one another. Have you learned how to be your partner's biggest "cheerleader?" Learn how to support your partner's dreams, goals, and aspirations in all stages of life. Put forth a strong effort to understand what your partner wants to do in their life. Doing so will allow you to not become a "Debbie Downer" to their dreams. There is nothing worse than a partner attempting to do what is best for their hopes and dreams but constantly dealing with a partner who is combative, due to a lack of understanding. If your partner has to make a decision related to work that you truly don't understand, don't make their decision about you—never hold them back.

Make Your Significant Other's Dreams Just as Important as Your Aspirations. A relationship is destined to fail if you are not dedicated to the dreams of your lover as if they were your own. As one part of a couple, make it a priority that both parties are enthusiastically working toward respective goals. You should be working to create a shared vision with your partner. Soon, both of you will be completely invested in each other's ambitions.

Become Their "Personal Cheerleader." Enthusiasm and words of encouragement toward your partner's road to success will absolutely make them feel as if they are on top of the world.

Go out of your way to congratulate your significant other when they are conquering their goals. You should be ecstatic that your romantic counterpart is working to be a success, so express those feelings! Take time to write personal notes applauding your lover's accomplishments. Physically become a part of their achievement when possible. Let them know that they are doing a great job. If you are not able to physically tell your partner how happy their accomplishment made you, a quick phone call will suffice in that moment. You have no idea how the aforementioned suggestions will positively register with your partner.

Help the Love of Your Life Achieve. Get in the habit of asking, "How can I help?" Yes, we are aware that most couples do not share professional interests but don't let that hinder you. The goal is to be an extra set of hands, not to be a contributing team member of their project. Your partner will appreciate you being there for them in a time of need.

> *Elle-Woods Personal Note from Alvin: We do our best to assist each other whenever possible. Fortunately, Antonio and I have career paths that complement one another. As a publicist and brand manager, I do my best to make sure that my husband is networking with people who can influence his budding artistic career. There have also been times when he has introduced me to an entrepreneur looking to build a buzz for a new brand. We have an understanding that if he succeeds, so do I. Most successful people have a dynamic partner at their side—be that forceful counterpart for your significant other.*

Be Prepared to Pick 'Em Up if They Fall. Learn to empathize with your partner and provide encouragement when they are feeling down. You have to be prepared at all times to weather the personal storm of your counterpart.

If your partner feels as if their world is crumbling, you have to reprioritize energy and immediately jump into their mindset. Even though you are in the same mental space, highlight an optimistic thought process. That positive eternal support will forever be valued. Imagine how much of an intense connection the two of you will develop as romantic partners. There's nothing sexier than a supportive spouse.

CHAPTER III

R.E.S.P.E.C.T.
and
Appreciate Me

The ideal marriage is dependent on respecting your partner for who they are as an individual. It's imperative to show constant appreciation for the love of your life. You have to hold your partner in the highest regard and give them all the impartiality that they deserve.

Empowerment is Love. To love your partner is to empower them. Think about it—the most substantial gift that you can give your romantic counterpart is uplifting their spirit. Being a part of a successful union will indeed give both parties a sense of authority and responsibility to respect one another.

A major first step to empowering your partner is to truly accept them. The utmost respect is to at no time ever want to change the personality or character of your significant other. You made a conscious decision at the beginning of your romantic journey to love someone for the person that they were in that particular moment, so let them be. When you hold your partner at the highest regard, it will allow continued growth in their direction of choice.

A certain level or respect for the person you love will make or break your ideal union. Hopefully you and your partner are, at the very least, on the cusp of making the romantic merger work. If so, you are well on your way to living the dream that you want with your significant other. If not, there is much emotional work that needs to be done. Don't feel defeated, just put in the effort.

Express How Much You Value Your Relationship. There can never be too much emphasis put on how much you appreciate the relationship that is being built with both you and your partner. "The little things" should always be the most important aspect of a solid marriage. Do your best to make your partner feel appreciated every day. Treat them to sporadic "I Love You" or "Thank You for Being You" moments, just because. Small thoughtful gestures will absolutely make your partner's day as it shows your significant other that you are thinking of both them and your relationship. We're not saying that you need to devote every moment to pampering your mate but a great token of affection once-in-a-while goes a long way.

Always remember that neither you nor your partner has done each other a favor by being in a relationship together. If you are constantly feeling as if you are doing some sort of charity work in a partnership, your energy is in the wrong place and you may need to reconsider your motives.

Reciprocity. Relationships are all about a mutual effort of give and take. Both parties have to cooperate with one another to not only achieve a successful partnership but also to accomplish individual life goals.

Learn how to reciprocate positive energy and admiration for one another. There should never be an instance where one person in a relationship constantly depletes the energy of another. Some days you may need to fully support your partner but there will definitely be times when you need that attention as well. Have those important conversations with your partner in which you state what you need from them. You should never be surprised by what your partner will provide to you emotionally.

Elle-Woods Personal Note from Antonio: Our relationship is an ongoing learning process and we have educated each other on how to be more pleasant to not only each other but also to others in which we come into contact. Being upbeat with a sense of understanding to those around us on a regular basis allows a cheerful domestic atmosphere. Now we effortlessly reciprocate a strong appreciation and mutual respect for one another. Our house is filled with polite gestures such as "please" and "thank you."

CHAPTER IV

Come and Talk to Me

We've all heard that communication in a relationship is important but open conversation and dialogue about all topics, without judgment, is the "blood line" to an ideal marriage. You should be married to your best friend so why would there be any secrets or topics that are off limits?

Listen with a Non-Judgmental Heart. Extreme importance must be put on empathizing with your partner. A crucial element of any successful relationship and marriage is to understand the feelings of your significant other. This act of compassion will eliminate judgment and serves as an integral key to open and honest conversation between the both of you.

Always remember that it isn't your place to judge your partner. Keep in mind that you will need their ear at some point and will not feel like fully expressing yourself if you feel as if your thoughts are being dissected.

Elle-Woods Personal Note from Alvin: Remember to regularly immerse yourself in listening when your partner speaks. I've learned to make my husband feel as if there is nothing more important than what he is saying. This learning has been substantial for me because in that moment, there is truly nothing more important than what's going on in his mind and heart. It has been my obligation to ensure my partner that I should be the first person he wants to talk too and confide within.

Your Secrets are Safe with Me. Do you remember how you told your closest friends everything as a child? Now that you are in a committed relationship, your partner should be that number one confidant at all times. Develop a "safe zone" during conversations with your significant other so that they are comfortable having intimate conversations with you.

Seriously, if your spouse isn't comfortable talking to you, who will they confide in when there is a need to do so? Do your best to make sure that your significant other knows exactly where their secrets are being stored.

Nothing off Limits. Your "safe zone" has already been established so hopefully the two of you are building a rapport in which all topics are up for discussion. You should be able to talk openly with your partner about insecurities and fears in the same way that goals and dreams are discussed. Yes, it may be difficult at times to open up about certain topics but the beauty of a successful romantic partnership is that you have an around-the-clock buddy for pillow talk. If you cannot communicate throughout the day, find time to talk on a daily basis. Never allow your emotions or thoughts on any topic to fester within. Encourage one another to become an "open book" as solid communication builds character of a relationship. It is so liberating to know that you can be as expressive as you want to be with your life partner.

CHAPTER V

Hey,
I'm on
Your Team!

A solid marriage or relationship will never work if each person involved holds onto their individual ego. We all take frustrations out on the people that are closest to us but we must refrain from treating our significant other negatively without merit. Taking cheap shots at your partner when you are angry does nothing but put unnecessary cracks in the foundation that the two of you are building. Treat your romantic relationship as if it is you and that person against the rest of the world.

I'm Not Your Enemy. Take note—The two of you are on the same team; there is no need to tear your partner down so that you feel better. Losing your temper happens but as an adult, it is up to you to control yourself. Never resort to physical abuse or continuously remind your significant other of their faults by re-introducing old problems that caused a dispute. If you are with the right person, you will feel personal disgust that you sunk low enough to tear down your only teammate.

It can be way too easy to hit your partner below the belt when you are angry. Always remember that minor domestic spats will end and there will be no love lost between the two of you. Know that every couple will argue and have challenges but do your best as a team to not let family and friends know your trials—prepare to solve the quarrel amongst the two of you.

Words Hurt. Do your absolute best to think about what you say to your significant other when you are upset. This tip is by far one of the most difficult in which to follow through. In the moment you may be thinking that since you are hurting, you want your partner to feel pain as well. This approach will get you nowhere.

Many people say hurtful things to their significant other in order to create a false sense of happy within. If your other half is slinging hateful words toward you, don't join in on the degrading party. Distasteful words thrown at each other during an argument will continuously play back in your mind and can be detrimental to a progressive relationship. Just as physical abuse is not appropriate, verbal abuse should also be locked away in a box never to be opened. Precious intimate encounters are what brought you to this current point in your life. Take the past as learning experiences that ultimately led to your new happy state of being. Never recreate negative moments, because all that you will be left with are sad memories.

You must uplift your partner through words. Never orally assault them to the point that they feel defeated. Remember that your tone does indeed matter! It may be too difficult for your partner to focus on what you are actually saying because of the way you are saying it.

You're Hostile but Identify the Real Issue. Arguments tend to escalate due to an underlying issue that has nothing to do with the current disagreement. Put aside your pride in the moment to pinpoint why you are truly angry. Feel out your partner's energy and connect with them through the dispute. Grow closer as a couple after petty arguments take a turn for the worse by identifying the root of an argument.

Elle-Woods Personal Note from Alvin: We've learned the hard way that repressing personal issues can become an explosive contention if gone untreated.

With that being said, it may not be the best idea in a heated moment to ask your partner, "What's the real problem?" Make sure that the both of you are ready to get down to the real business at hand. An angry partner will think that you are attempting to change the subject if you blatantly as "What's the real problem?" This can actually spark a newly minted issue-of-the-moment.

Pride can ruin a relationship and be one of the major causes of a failed marriage. You must learn what loving someone wholeheartedly means—you are vulnerable enough to allow that person to hurt you but know they will not do so intentionally. Even though your ego can affect the way that you process emotions sparked by love, stay in tune with your conscience as that inner voice will never lead you astray.

Let Down Your Guard. Your partner loves you! He or she developed an emotional connection with you based on the person presented to them during your courting season. Allow your emotional light to shine. You owe it to your significant other to let them into your deepest and sincere thoughts. Essentially, your ego won't allow you to be great in a relationship—making it difficult to deal with feelings as if you are out of control. Reality check—you fell in love, that's why you feel out of control. The trick is to revel in that emotion, not to fight it.

Elle-Woods Personal Note from Antonio: From the beginning of my relationship with Alvin, I've had to aggressively work on letting down the barricade to my vulnerable heart. Thankfully, my husband-to-be at the time, was diligent enough to put up with my tough attitude which was caused by holding onto the memories of what other men had done to me in previous relationships. Chasing my happily-ever-after before meeting the love of my life took a toll on me. I'm fortunate to have had an epiphany that made me realize how much character I would be gaining by relinquishing the guards around my heart.

Lose the "You," Gain an "Us." In the moment that you made the decision to journey through life with your special someone, it was also decided to let go of the "you." Don't fret—the bonus is that you gained an "us!" An ideal relationship focuses on moving both parties forward with the same vigor as if it were one individual. Your partner will love when you use "us" and "our" versus "me" and "mine." In the right relationship, you should be able to easily transition into a collective unit alongside your partner. With that being said, don't worry if you are having difficulties converting your "you" into an "us." Some people's ego will delay a fluid shift but you will come around.

Get Out of Your Own Way. Don't allow your ego to combat your significant other in any way. Seriously, get out of your own way so that your ideal relationship can flourish! Since we both have had to individually fight our respective egos, we have come up with three ways to check that prideful attitude.

Number One: Don't be afraid to ask for help when needed. People enter a relationship as an independent force and do not know how to lean on their romantic counterpart once a union has been formed. The only opinion that matters once you find your perfect match is the opinion of that person and no one else. Your partner will not view you as inferior if you ask for assistance. Relationships are all about strengthening one another through helping each other.

Number Two: Live in the moment with your significant other. It's very easy to get lost in your own head when dealing with the stresses of your individual life. An understanding partner will allow moments to vent about stress at work or divulge how much you are dissatisfied with a person or service in which you received. Do not take that understanding partner for granted. Even the most empathetic person will begin to resent you for putting all of your attention into what ails you. At the end of the day, you have a special someone to get you through the proverbial storms. There are only twenty-four hours in a day—make them count!

Number Three: Learn to admit when you are wrong. Want to be let in on a little secret? You will not always be right. I hope we didn't hurt your ego with that revelation. Don't invest so much energy into trying to evoke your opinions and ideas as law onto your partner. Hopefully you are in a relationship with a person who can form their own opinions. Learn to be aware and responsive to your significant other when you are indeed wrong. Your partner not only expects you to value their opinion but should also demand that you are a rational adult during a disagreement. Want to be let in on another little secret? It's actually boring to always be right.

CHAPTER VI

The Glue

Trust in both your partner and relationship is arguably the only prerequisite in a successful relationship. Interdependence and sharing responsibility is a thriving force for two people that are romantically involved. It is not wise to enter the union of a marriage if there are doubts that you can trust the person in which you are marrying.

Marriage Prerequisite. Trusting in your partner is an absolute must and is extremely important when deciding that you want to be married. Some people enter romantic relationships with mistrust, requiring that their partner prove themselves to be worthy before trust is given. This is not usually the best way to start a partnership. Your initial intent should be to give your significant other the benefit of the doubt. Although you may be cautious, it is imperative to start a relationship on a positive note.

No one wants to be immediately suspected of wrong doing. The element of trust affects the livelihood of every relationship and should be as fluid as water between two people that love one another.

Honesty. Loyalty. Dedication. Your partner's main objective should always be honesty. It's your responsibility to honor the vows that you have taken under the bond of marriage. Luxuriate in the glory of being married. It is important that the people in which you come into contact with know you are happily in a committed relationship. A good spouse is loyal and dedicated to their partner. Continuously showing that you are not only honest, loyal, and dedicated to your marriage will forever build a foundation of trust that will never be able to be broken.

The vows of marriage are an intimate pledge that should be upheld at all times.

Solve Problems Together, Change Your Reality. Take time to learn the art of problem solving together. A relationship can be a bed of roses before you say "I do," but can quickly wilt when challenges come about. It's not healthy or fair for one person in a union to make all the hard decisions in a long-term partnership. Learn along with your significant other to do what is best for the family structure as a collective unit. Do your partner a favor by not becoming a burden to problems that are now hurdles for your family. As a couple, take on the weight of the world as one, knowing that your shared beliefs will change your joint reality.

Openly Discuss Financial Challenges and Opportunities. The ideal romantic relationship can only be so if that union is a solid financial business partnership as well. Most couples will have challenges regarding past debts, bills, and spending. The key is to become comfortable with each other in order to discuss how the both of you will handle money. Yes, we know that discussing money may be extremely difficult for you to do with your partner but think about this—money matters to an extent and the well-being of your relationship depends on how you both handle financial challenges as well as opportunities. How can you expect everlasting bliss with your partner if money is not discussed? Here's a tip to keep your relationship thriving—Be open about the amount of money you both earn. It will become even more difficult to stay within budgetary constraints if you are less than straightforward regarding the amount of coin that comes into the household. Always remember this—a happy spouse keeps you in the house!

Develop Timelines to Attain Goals. In order to make substantial progress toward your goals as a couple, you and your partner should absolutely invest into creating timelines to attain goals.

> *Elle-Woods Personal Note from Alvin: My husband and I are by no means financial experts but we have concluded that developing timelines to attain both our personal and collective financial goals are important to our happy union. As two independent men, it wasn't easy to fully disclose our individual finances and compromise on how to achieve goals but after creating a template for financial freedom we are now life-long business partners. We work together to make sure that one day our lives are on track to be as secure as possible.*

Make Appointments to Talk About Domestic Burdens. It's important to talk about all challenges with your significant other without hesitation. Solve problems with a sense of urgency. Go about doing what is best for your partnership and arrange daily or weekly meetings between the two of you if necessary. Don't carry the weight of a challenge by yourself. One of the perks of an ideal marriage or relationship is that you do not have to do it alone!

When your spouse comes to you with a challenge, have an opinion on the matter. Make it your responsibility to brainstorm ideas as well as come up with decisions to help your significant other through a rough patch. In order to do so, you must be able to deal with your own stress. This will indeed take unwanted pressure off of your marriage.

CHAPTER VII

Royalty,
Walking Side by Side—
Keeping it Haute

The days of couples playing the "I'm superior and you're inferior" game is over! The twenty-tens is a decade that has seen the rise of equal counterparts in relationships so why should dominate roles still exist? Couples should treat each other like royalty and depend on each other for all aspects of a marriage.

> *Elle-Woods Personal Note from Alvin: We're two kings, walking side by side and know that our reign together will be impactful and full of purpose. As a couple we understand how much of an honor it is to journey through this life with each other. We rightfully wear our individual crowns and make no apologies for doing so. Although some people may think that this idea is a bit pretentious, we believe that "wearing our crowns" is humbling because we only have a powerful reign when we are together.*

Even though you have made a life-long commitment to your partner, forget about the relationship going the distance without some serious nurturing and attention. Preserving the "hauteness" in a partnership has to do with maintaining an elevated level of *you* for your significant other.

Build Confidence in Your King or Queen. Letting your partner know just how desirable they are to you is an ultimate confidence booster for them. Go out of your way to compliment your spouse. When they are getting ready to go out with friends, spoil them with compliments. When your significant other gets home from a long day at work, make their arrival a main event. If your partner does something different to their appearance, shower them with affirmation that they've never looked better. Regardless of your spouse's self-esteem, positive confirmations will make them feel better about themselves. If you can make your significant other feel as if they are truly the one that does *it* for you, your connection will be strengthened by leaps and bounds.

Another way to enhance confidence in your romantic counterpart is to tell him or her often that you love them but more importantly *why* you love them. If done with a genuine heart, the gesture will come across as thoughtful and refreshing every time. You should want a partner that is confident and proud to be by your side. Only you can give them the assurance needed to walk with such strength.

Maintain a Dating Phase. Most couples don't think that it is important to stay in a dating phase with the love of your life—This is a crucial mistake, now fix it! Why should that euphoric feeling during the dating phase of your relationship end? In the beginning you were accustomed to your relationship being on a pedestal for the world to see. It's natural for that exhilarating feeling to lose some steam but here's a tip to stay in that dating bliss—hold onto the appreciation felt for your lover on the first day in which you realized that person was *the one.* Go back to the moment when you wanted to spend every waking breath with your precious gem of a partner.

Even when life gets in the way, holding on to those moments will allow you to show your love and as often as possible. Whether people want to admit it or not, we are all excited when someone we love is affectionate toward us. Maintaining that loving charm with one another will prolong that honeymoon phase for a lifetime.

Luxuriate in the Small Things. Love your partner in all of their quirky glory! Learn to focus on what you admire about your significant other and value the time that you two spend together. Elevate your partner by showering him or her with tokens of affection. It is such a wonderful feeling to be loved. Make your spouse feel as if they don't have to lift a finger. Those gestures by you will surely be noticed and your significant other will do the same for you.

It's a must to indulge in your relationship with your partner. The two of you should be constantly touching if in close proximity. We absolutely don't mean that you should make people uncomfortable with obscene public displays of affection but a hand on the knee or a soothing caress of the arm will always suffice.

Take moments throughout the day to whisper "sweet nothings" in their ear and steal seconds when other people are in the room by gazing at each other like no one else is around. Know that your relationship is extraordinary when you can be in an area filled with colleagues, friends or family, and you are able to make the room disappear to only see your romantic counterpart. Simply put, cherish each other with spontaneous affection. You can never reinforce your commitment to your partner enough.

No Need to Remember How if Used to Be. Keeping the spark is often a job within a job. In your professional career you are supposed to find something that you love to do and it won't seem like work. In a relationship, the same rule applies—find someone you love unconditionally and you won't feel like keeping the passion between the two of you is work.

At the start of your courtship, hopefully you enjoyed your significant other for both their inner and outer appeal. Both of you should aim to be all that you be. This does not mean that women have to live up to the beauty standards of a super model and men have to be the spitting image of an A-list actor, it just means that you should have pride in your appearance. No adult wants to be embarrassed by their significant other while out in public. Whether your relationship is fresh and new or older and slightly less-new, exert some energy to look your best when out with your counterpart. Pajamas are fine while in the house but have no purpose outside other than to go check the mail. The biggest mistake that you can make in a relationship is to let yourself go—there, we said it! I know that it may be hard to hear this startling revelation but some people need to hear it. Keep it haute. Your significant other will appreciate it.

CHAPTER VIII

*Peppermint Kisses,
Comedic Relief
and Spontaneity*

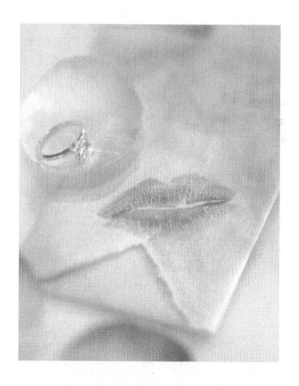

Peppermint Kiss. Peppermint is known to enhance memory and people in relationships need to hit the refresh button at times. Are you reading to find a tip that will directly enhance the physical connection in your romantic partnership? We hope to provide a moment of clarity that will indeed change your perception regarding your ideal union. The "peppermint kiss" is a sensual embrace shared between partners and should happen once a day, at the very least. The passionate kiss between lovers will remind both parties how much they are actually attracted to one another.

Albeit we are intentionally focusing on the emotional and mental ways to connect with your partner and are restraining to talk about the physical act of making love, think of the "peppermint kiss" like this—The doozy of an intimate exchange that leads to sex or the type of passionate exchange that happens during sex! Whew, we just got excited but back to the point at hand. Take time out of your day to make your partner remember how good the physical sex is between the two of you.

> *Elle-Woods Personal Note from Antonio: My husband and I work on our relationship to ensure that we both have had our last, first kiss. We have even taken our devotion as far as creating K.I.S.S.I.N.G. rituals. We absolutely look forward to Christmas and Valentine's Day season, not for the exchanging of gifts but for commercials by the number one specialty jewelry brand, Kay Jewelers. We make it our business to kiss every time the voice-over on one of the television ads utters the iconic tagline, "Every kiss begins with Kay."*

This is an example of one of the many eccentricities that we share and love.

The Supremacy of Laughter. Fun and laughter are an essential aspect to barricade potential stress in a relationship. Life is too difficult at times and you should find humor in everyday situations. Doing so will allow both you and your partner to lighten up and have a good time. Did you know that laughter can relax the entire body, protect the heart, and boost your immune system? You may be able to argue that a daily vitamin isn't needed when you're in a positive and healthy relationship because laughing with your significant other is the best medicine for what ails you.

Don't let your daily routine slow your growth and put you in a rut. When you are down, watch a funny movie together. If the day has been a bit gloomy, find the energy to act silly around the house together. Challenge yourself to maintain a sense of humor through the ups, and more importantly, the downside during your journey. Work to laugh every day as often as possible—you will thank us later. Find someone who doesn't like to laugh and we will show you someone who takes life too seriously.

Surprise! Sometimes it can be quite a task to find time to nourish the friendship with your spouse. If you both work full-time it is worth the effort to spontaneously enjoy one another. Here's a way to have some spur-of-the-moment fun—surprise him or her! Even if your significant other claims to not like surprises, that just means that they don't know how to accept the seemingly impulsive act of kindness. Do not let their apprehension stop you.

A surprise can be anything from organizing a birthday party they are not aware of, or planning a night out with friends when you know that they have been stressed. You can even surprise your romantic counterpart with their favorite candy or food at work.

Other ways to be spontaneous is to cook hands-on meals together, play your favorite games while enjoying cocktails and see where the night takes the two of you, or even learning a new hobby together. The trick is to have as much fun with the love of your life, as it is a luxury to do so. You are spending time with your best friend and should make every moment count. If you find yourself immediately stumped for ideas, start your week with a brainstorm session to figure out what you can do to make the upcoming days special for your significant other. Once you have accomplished your goal, have another brainstorm session to create the next special moment.

CHAPTER IX

Compromise for Your Happy

Let's be real—if you are looking for someone to boss around and make all of their decisions, get a damn dog. A true relationship is about learning to compromise but we live in a society in which compromising can be considered weak in the eyes of our peers. The real problem is that we attempt to live by what society deems appropriate *and for* the respect of our peers. Although it may not be easy for you to comprehend, your relationship should never be a one-sided arrangement. We are not saying that you are guilty of this but if you are constantly dictating to your partner—stop it. Yes, you are in a relationship but this does not mean that you have ownership of your significant other. It is one thing to care about the well-being of your partner but it's a completely different topic when you command their every move. Compromising with one another is an ongoing learning process.

Your Partner's Well-Being. Questions that a person may ask themselves during the beginning of a relationship are valid—*How will I benefit financially? How can this partnership assist my climb up the social ladder? What about me?* Although necessary questions to a certain extent, you need to start asking yourself similarly important questions in a different way—*How am I making a financial contribution to this partnership? Are we reaching the professional and personal goals on our agenda? What about us?*

Individuals that enter a relationship usually do so for their own welfare and that's okay for a certain amount of time. We are all in need of certain comforts to feel valuable but at some point in your romantic journey, you have to fundamentally shift your motives. As one half of a partnership, you must care for your significant other's livelihood as much as your own. In an ideal union, you will begin to think of your partner's happiness, health, and mental stability more than your own. The great news—the right companion will do the same for you! It is never wise to give so much of yourself to a person that will not provide a similar responsibility.

Meet in the Middle. Follow Through with a Smile. You can look forward to countless times that you will have no desire to participate in doing something or going somewhere with your significant other. Most of the time, just go with the flow. A considerate partner will not only suggest doing what they want to do all of the time but also ask what you want to do. Think of how your relationship will grow when you partake in an activity that you normally would not want to do. It's important to constantly build a companionship by sharing in a hobby or common interest. You'll never know how much you could enjoy an activity until you try. Even if you are not having the most fun, appeasing your significant other should make the event or hobby enticing.

If you find yourself completely unenthused with an activity suggested by your partner, follow through with a smile. You've already decided to participate so don't spend a lot of time complaining. Make the best out of the situation and be positive throughout the experience. You might find yourself in a stale mood at times because compromising with anyone, especially the one you love, is never easy. Come out of a decision making process feeling as if you've lost. You may be confused by our previous statement because it might sound strange but if both parties feel like they lost the compromise, it was a true negotiation.

> *Elle-Woods Personal Note from Alvin: I have a strong personality. My husband has a strong personality. I'm more of a social butterfly who wants to enjoy activities outside of our home. My husband is quite content enjoying more activities in our home unless work is involved. I try my best to compromise for my happy because everything that I want to do isn't appealing to my husband. I give him complete freedom to not partake in my random walks around New York City. As a Southern transplant, there is nothing better to me than walking around Gotham seeing the beauty of this amazing city—the architecture, the millions of people and amazing cultures. As a native New Yorker, there isn't much outside that impresses my husband. If it's not a nice dinner or musical, he needs a bit of coaching and persuading. My artistic husband is a film connoisseur and can watch a movie, on what seems like, constant repeat. Let's just say that I've seen more movies in the last year than I have seen in my entire life.*

Don't dictate to your partner. Never attempt to act as a parental figure to your significant other. Enjoy them in their element as they will learn to enjoy you in your comfort zone. Choose activities or hobbies together. We know that compromising is not easy. As a couple, you have to learn how to have fun! Compromising for your happy will ensure a stronger relationship! Live your life to the fullest with your significant other.

CHAPTER X

Balance This,
Balance That

It's absolutely imperative to maintain a healthy balance for your relationship so that you can maintain a happy equilibrium. As it is important to make time for the love of your life, you must also balance work, personal time and family along with couple time. The trick is to nurture both your romantic relationship as well as everything else that makes you unique. Continue to develop new interests and socialize as we all are forever evolving.

The Hierarchy of Balance. Although your partner is the most important person in your life, there may be family members and dear friends in which you want to divvy up your time. The hierarchy has everything to do with prioritizing what's important from day-to-day. In a relationship, your significant other should always get top billing. With that being said, there is more than enough of you to go around.

Abraham Maslow's *Hierarchy of Needs* breaks down the fundamental levels best—Physiological, Safety, Social (Love/Belonging), Esteem, and Self-Actualization. If you are having difficulty finding a balance, use the following as a guide.

- Top-Tier Priorities: Spouse/Significant Other, Immediate Family, and Work
- Secondary Priorities: Extended Family and Friends
- Tertiary Priorities: Creativity and Acceptance of Others

Never Lose Out on Being Yourself. In an ideal partnership, you must trade in the "I" for "We," which is dutifully noted but individual identities are an essential factor that leads to a strong marriage. The best significant others have their own distinct interests.

Do your best to maintain a social calendar. If your partner works more hours than you do or has projects that take up potential couple time, don't become frustrated with him or her—follow suite. Remember, you embarked on this relationship to be happy. Don't become upset because you are waiting for your partner to fill a social void in your life. It's great that the two of you are best buddies but even the closest of friends don't spend *every* free moment with each other. When you began your romantic journey, you had your own life and to a certain level, that should not be altered. Continue to do many of the productive things that you love as you should not give up seeing friends or lose out on doing your favorite extracurricular activities. Incorporate your significant other when time allows but stay in touch with *you*. Doing so will create a substantially happier "We."

Don't Be Selfish. GIVE. YOUR. PARTNER. SPACE. If you are in the right relationship, you may want to spend every waking moment with your significant other. Even though that's a great feeling, do your best to not become selfish with your better-half's time. You are the center of your partner's world but everything they do does not revolve around you. Hopefully you are with a well-rounded person who has a loving family and career, are passionate about certain activities and hobbies, as well as have influential friends and colleagues in their life. Don't always expect total undivided attention from your significant other.

If he or she has hobbies and friends, allow them time to enjoy other people and interests that make them happy. Just because they are enjoying themselves does not mean that they don't want you around. Do not be vindictive toward your partner by trying to make them feel guilty about spending some of their free time with friends or business associates. It's unfair to assume that your partner has to be at your side at all times. Why ruin their fun by throwing a tantrum when the want to socialize? Being selfish with your partner's time will only make them resent you. As long as your partner is taking care of top-tier priorities, they should have the freedom to enjoy themselves from time-to-time.

Once a week or every-other-week, allow your partner to enjoy time with friends or delve into a hobby that isn't affiliated with work. Giving him or her respect to enjoy themselves without you around does not give them the authority to party hard all the time. It will reassure your partner that you value them as a person—as friendships and hobbies outside of couple time are important aspects to an ideal relationship.

Elle-Woods Personal Note from Alvin: If you have plans that don't necessarily include your significant other, ask them if they would like to attend. I've learned that on occasions, spending time with friends without asking my husband if he wanted to come along with me has made him feel left out. The sheer gesture of asking your partner if he or she wants to accompany you will mean the world to them. With that being said, be prepared for your spouse to say that they want to go with you. A rational partner will know when to decline the offer.

CHAPTER XI

Hopelessly Devoted

Our love is a beautiful, overwhelming moment in time that is punctuated by pure bliss. We are hopelessly and deeply devoted to making our romantic union stand the test of time. Our cosmic journey started over three years ago with a chance meeting and through several trials and tribulations, it was evident that we were meant to be. Love found us and we didn't let it go.

This collection of tips, thoughts, and learnings were compiled from our personal experiences and will always be used as a template to make our relationship the healthy union we hope it will continue to be. Often times, couples put way too much emphasis on the physical aspect of a relationship, allowing the emotional and mental connections to fade. It is our hope that *The Best Workout is "Sex": A Gay Guide to Your Ideal Marriage* has enlightened you and provided clarity on how to strengthen the connection with your partner—whether you are in a relationship with someone of the opposite sex or romantically journeying through life with another person of the same-sex.

Although some of us fight every day to simply live our lives, this day and age confidently allows us all to push a bit harder to thrive in our own truth. We should all be thankful for a world of continued inclusion and acceptance. For over a decade, the issue a same-sex marriage, domestic partnerships, and civil unions have been a hot button topic in the United States. As of March 1, 2012, eight states as well as District of Columbia have legalized same-sex marriage in the United States. With that being said, opponents are collecting signatures for an attempt to repeal the newly-signed law in Maryland.

We are a couple that has been able to benefit from a human right, granted to us in New York City on July 24, 2011. The specific Sunday conceded us to be trailblazers for those who have long argued that marriage is a distinctive expression of commitment as well as love, and anything else could easily be viewed as a second-class citizenship. For that moment, we are forever grateful.

Regardless of what you think about people like us whose sexual orientation may be different from yours, we all have a common denominator when dealing with relationships—the power of love. Whether you are in a heterosexual relationship or in a committed same-sex relationship, use our guidelines to find your happy—always be attentive, compassionate, and communicative with your partner. Never forget to love yourself, support and appreciate one another, check your ego, wrap your relationship in trust, keep it haute, enjoy peppermint kisses, laugh, and maintain a healthy balance throughout life.

If we are able to help just one couple find their happiness, we have met our goal. You may have set qualifications for your ideal love but we hope that you have truly found the person who is the exception to all of your rules. Love without limitations.

Now that you have learned how to have amazing mental and emotional "sex" from this gay guide to your ideal marriage, go off and connect with your partner.

Afterword

A Personal Letter from Antonio to Alvin:

"People want to fall in love . . . people look for love but you, my love, found me. You are more than just my best friend you are my new life. God has made you for me and I'm so blessed to have gone through all of the things in my life to have found you. I was always looking for love in all of the wrong places but never really knew how to love myself.

Before meeting you, I was deeply tired from situations that happened in life and wanted it all to just to end. You took the time out to study me and learn me in ways that I never thought any person could. You took my heart and put it together with just a smile. Our kisses tell me that I have found my perfect match. You push me to be better because you see something no one else has ever seen in me. No matter what I'm going through you always find a way to make me laugh. I know that in my heart our love is unworldly . . .

I promise to keep you happy for as long as we live. I promise to honor you and respect you as my partner, my best friend, and my soul mate. I thank you for being by my side when no one else was there. I thank you for staying by my side through it all. Thank you for taking my cold hand and making it warm again; for taking my cold heart and warming it with LOVE. I'm blessed to be everything to you. It's me and you baby. I love you . . . This is our love and no one can take that from us. Elle-Woods. Lopez-Woods, forever."

After reading this, how can anyone deny our love? After reading this, how can anyone blatantly deny human rights to people that feel the same way about their partner, who may just be of the same-sex? Some people love in different ways. Some people have different religious beliefs. The beauty of life is that we are all uniquely diverse.

ABOUT THE AUTHORS

Alvin and Antonio Lopez-Woods are a happily married couple based in New York City that advocate love and respect are vital to any union, regardless of gender and sexual orientation. The two made history as one of the first same-sex couples to legally marry in the Empire State.

Reference

Maslow, A. (n.d.) Maslow's Hierachy of Needs. *Abraham Maslow Father of Modern Management.* Retrieved January 6, 2012, from *http://www.abraham-maslow. com/m_motivation/Hierarchy_of_Needs.asp.*